Mutual Funds EXPOSED
What you don't know may be
hazardous to your wealth.

Kim | Nelson

EQIS Capital Management, Inc.
1000 4th Street
San Rafael, CA 94901
www.eqis.com

First Printing, 2014
ISBN 978-0-9908249-0-9
Library of Congress Control Number: 2014917565
Printed in the United States of America

The information contained herein is believed to be reliable but is neither guaranteed by EQIS Capital Management, Inc., its principals nor any affiliated EQIS companies. Content includes Dr. Kim's, Dr. Nelson's and EQIS' opinions and is not guaranteed. The information is intended for the exclusive use of licensed investment professionals. This is not a solicitation to buy or sell securities. CID 140313

Dedication

We dedicate this book to our children, Sophia, Hector, Ken, and David. Our love for you inspires us to invest wisely for your futures.

A note from the authors:

Because we wanted our book to have a conversational tone, the book is written in Dr. Kim's voice. However, the book was a collaborative effort by both Dr. Kim and Dr. Nelson.

Table of Contents

Forward

It gives me great pleasure to write the foreword to this important (and entertaining) book. The author, Ken Kim, is my good friend, and I have greatly benefited from picking his brain about investments for the past 20 years. But, more important, Dr. Kim is a world-renowned expert in finance. In fact, I've had the pleasure to collaborate with him on a finance trade book, a college textbook, and numerous scholarly finance articles. So I know that Ken is always passionate about exposing the inefficiencies and myths of financial markets and the financial industry. I am not surprised that he wrote this book. It needed to be done, and he is just the person to do it! I am really glad that he did, and you will be too.

Everyone holds mutual funds. We own them directly, through brokerage accounts, and in our defined contribution plans. Mutual funds have always had their flaws, but for many decades, they were often the best investment vehicle that we had. But today, this is no longer the case. The investment industry has evolved to produce better ways to invest. Why are mutual funds obsolete and flawed investments? There are many reasons, and Ken has done a fantastic job at illustrating and explaining them in an entertaining and easy-to-understand style. Specifically, you may be shocked to learn about hidden costs, unfair taxes, and unproductive diversification. Read this book! Then evolve your portfolio to secure your finances for the future.

— **Dr. John Nofsinger, PhD**, author of the popular book, *Investment Madness*, the industry staple, *The Psychology of Investing*, 5e, and the college textbook, *Investments: Analysis and Behavior.*

Preface

Remember when the only way we could call someone was with a phone that was literally attached to a wall in our home or office? Remember when we looked up words from a thick dictionary, listened to cassette tapes, typed on typewriters, wrote letters to friends with pencil and paper that took days to be delivered, got airline tickets delivered to us in the mail; remember when we drove around in new places with folded maps on our laps? There was even a time when we didn't know what a computer was. Today, we have smart phones, MP3s, the Internet, emails/texts, GPSs, tablets, and so on.

Because of technology, what we used to do in the past seems so funny to many of us today.

Also, remember when we used to be invested in mutual funds (hahaha, that was really funny), but now we can be in separately managed accounts? I still can't believe... ummm,... what? You don't know what I am talking about? Uh-oh, it looks like a part of you is still living in the past. If you are primarily invested in mutual funds, then you are behind the times, and I think you should read this book. Do it now! Before it's too late!

Mutual funds can suffer from many flaws. Many of these flaws may impose costs that are not always disclosed to you, including tax inefficiency (see Chapter 2), high "hidden" costs (see Chapter 3), and high management costs (see Chapter 4). Mutual funds might also underperform (see Chapter 4), suffer from over-diversification (see Chapter 5), and may be nontransparent (see Chapter 6), and, sadly, they may even be sneaky (see Chapter 7).

But fear not. There is a simple alternative: Separately Managed Accounts (SMAs) (see Chapter 8). I hope you will read this book. It's in plain language, it's non-technical, it's informative, and I even tried to make it fun to read (but I probably failed in this last regard). But, most important, it may help you to secure your financial dreams.

Welcome to the 21st century way of investing. By the way, have you heard about those cars that can drive themselves? I need to look into that....

Chapter One
Introduction

By now, you may have heard or have read many times that buying a mutual fund can be a flawed and outdated way to invest.

Perhaps the two most common reasons given for why mutual funds are bad investments is because of their opaque and high fees (i.e., you get charged a lot, but you have no idea why) and because they are notoriously known to underperform benchmarks such as the S&P 500 index. There's actually much, much more to it than this. In fact, especially with today's technology, investing in mutual funds can be an archaic, costly, and inappropriate way to invest.[1]

Much of the problems with mutual funds stem from the fact that mutual fund firms own the stocks and bonds in the mutual fund and that you as an investor can really only purchase "a claim" on the fund, but you do not literally own any stocks or bonds in the fund. Instead, the mutual fund companies own the stocks and bonds for you, and they also own them for the many other people who buy the same mutual funds before you and after you. That is, your investment is "commingled" with other investors. What a weird arrangement. This means that when you buy a mutual fund today, and your fund owns Google stock, which is priced at, let's say, $500 per share, it does not count as though you bought Google stock at this price today, because you literally did not buy Google stock today. Instead, you bought a fund today that bought Google stock a while ago. This is confusing, right? Well, maybe the mutual fund industry likes it when you're confused if they can get you to invest in their funds. So, why is it so bad to be a commingled investor in a mutual fund? It can actually be a big problem for you. This book will help expose many of the reasons. We'll start with what many consider to be one of the biggest flaws of mutual funds: their tax inefficiency.

Chapter 1 Endnotes:

[1] Mutual funds as outdated or flawed investments is written about frequently. For example, see:

❖ Fabian, D. (2009, February 15). Mutual funds are hazardous to your wealth. Retrieved from http://www.marketwatch.com/story/investors-mutual-funds-hazardous-your-wealth.

❖ Guillot, C. (2013, March 11). Will mutual funds become obsolete? Retrieved from http://blog.betterinvesting/investing/will-mutual-funds-become-obsolete.

❖ Harris, B. (2013, June 20). The 10 biggest mutual funds: Are they really worth your money? Retrieved from http://www.forbes.com/sites/billharris/2012/08/08/the-10-biggest-mutual-funds-are-they-really-worth-your-money.

Chapter Two
Tax inefficiency of mutual funds

One reason why many experts say that investing in mutual funds is a flawed investment is because of its tax inefficiency. However, to be honest, I have never seen this flaw explained very well. For me, I need a simple numerical example to understand an abstract concept. So, if you're like me, then here's a numerical example that helps illustrate the tax inefficiency of mutual funds.

Let's say that you buy Monkey Mutual Fund today, and it has Banana Computer stock in it that is priced at $90 per share today. Later in the week, let's say that Banana stock price drops to $80/share (ouch, that's too bad for you), and the fund then decides to sell the stock. Now, get ready to be surprised. Let's say that the fund had bought Banana stock at $75/share. This means that the fund realizes a capital gain of $5/share (because it bought at $75/share and sold at $80/share), and thus pays a capital gains tax of, let's say, $1/share. This tax will probably come out of the fund's year-end distribution to their investors, including YOU.[2] How fair is this to you? Of course, I think it's not fair at all. Not only did you lose $10/share on Banana stock's value decline, but in effect you are also paying taxes on capital gains that you personally did not experience. Some of the fund's capital gains on Banana stock *might* go to you at the year-end distribution to all shareholders but note that a $5/share capital gain, net of $1/share expenditure in taxes, does not offset your actual experienced loss of $10/share.

At this point, you've got to be shocked (if you're not, then reread the previous paragraph). You might even find my illustration to be so unbelievable that you may feel that it cannot be true. Well, I invite you to take my numerical example and to show it to any mutual fund manager and ask her or him if and, if so, how my analysis is flawed. I am pretty sure he or she will respond in one of the following possible ways: (1) he or she will look dumbfounded; (2) he or she will offer you an explanation that is likely so confusing that you may not be able to understand it, but it's not because you're stupid; it's because the explanation may be too convoluted and vague; or (3) he or she will describe ways in which the problem that I am describing can be offset by the many other actions that the fund will take. For example, with regard to the latter, the fund manager might say that many other fund activities can occur so that the tax flaw that I am describing could be washed out. But, let's get real. Wouldn't you prefer that the tax flaw that I am describing simply didn't exist in the first place, so that offsetting actions don't need to be taken?!

Here's more proof that my numerical illustration describing mutual funds' tax flaw can be economically significant to you. In my numerical example, you actually deserve a tax *credit*. After all, you personally suffered a stock price drop of $10/share. So, if the capital gains tax is 20%, then you would deserve a $2/share tax credit for your loss. Ummm, how is the fund going to get this tax credit for you? Think about it. In this example, at the end of the day, it's only you, not the fund, who ends up experiencing an actual value loss when Banana stock price dropped in value. You see, for you personally, the relevant "reference price" of Banana stock is $90 per share, since this was the value of the stock when you bought the fund. However, in this example, your reference price of Banana stock is a nonfactor when the fund buys and sells Banana stock. So, not only did you lose $10 per share on Banana stock because of its stock price decline, but you are also deprived of a $2 per share tax credit.

Now, at this point, you might think that maybe I'm a clever guy and thus I am able to make up a clever contrived numerical example just to help support my argument that mutual funds can suffer from tax inefficiencies. I have two responses to this assertion. First, thank you for the compliment. Second, it is true that my numerical example is just one of maybe a million possible combinations of odd things that can happen with mutual holdings and activities. And, to be completely honest with you, there might be some odd situations and occurrences where oddities can work in your favor. But, again, let's get real. Wouldn't it be best to avoid these odd situations altogether?! This is your hard-earned savings that we're talking about. Do you want your savings to be subjected to a bunch of odd effects that you hope will all wash out in the end?

And finally, you don't have to take my word for it that some mutual funds suffer from tax inefficiencies. Just use Google and do a search on the phrase "mutual fund tax inefficiency" or "mutual fund tax flaw" and I bet that you'll get a bunch of hits. Actually, I'm going to do this right now, hold on… (5 minutes later)… yep, I got almost 10 million hits. And it's a good thing that I did the Google search, as I came across this nice little find that describes mutual fund tax inefficiencies from Morningstar's webpage:

> *Investors in conventional mutual funds can get stuck with a tax bill on their mutual fund holdings, even if they've lost money since they've held the fund* [hey, this is just like my numerical illustration!]… and they also have to pay taxes on all fund distributions, including capital gains, which occur *when a fund manager sells an underlying holding for more than its purchase price* [see, your own personal reference price of the fund's holding is not factored in anywhere!].[3]

The italics in the quote above are my emphasis. Oh, and uh, the underlined text in the quote above is also me, just in case you didn't catch that.

And here's some useful text from Wikipedia (what did we ever do before Wikipedia?) that explains the tax inefficiency succinctly:

> After purchasing mutual fund shares, an investor will have a tax liability for any net capital gains in the mutual fund portfolio, even if the investments the fund sold for a gain were purchased before the investor owned the shares of the fund. This is known as an "unearned capital gain," and has negative effect on the investor's return from his mutual fund investment.[4]

See, I wasn't making any of this up. Well, at this point, you may feel that the tax inefficiency of mutual funds is a sufficient enough reason for you to stop considering them as a viable investment option. If so, then no need to read further—you will find what I believe is a better investment alternative in **Chapter**

8: A simple straightforward alternative. Oh, but you might also consider taking a look at **Chapter 5: Mutual funds can over-diversify**, which I think is also a pretty interesting read. But, if you have nothing else to do, then feel free to read on. I've got other shocking reasons for why I believe mutual funds can be flawed and obsolete investments.

Chapter 2 Endnotes:

[2] Bergstresser, D. (2002). Do after-tax returns affect mutual fund inflows? *Journal of Financial Economics*, 63, 381–414.

[3] Rushkewicz Reichart, K. (2010, February 15). How tax-efficient is your mutual fund? Retrieved from http://news.morningstar.com/articlenet/article.aspx?id=308356.

[4] Separately managed account. (n.d.). Retrieved from http://en.wikipedia.org/wiki/Separately_managed_account.

Chapter Three
You can suffer costs because of other investors!

As I mentioned in Chapter 1, when you and others buy a mutual fund, then you are actually paying a mutual fund firm to own stocks for you. You don't own the stocks directly. Because mutual funds have many investors, including those who invested before you invested and those who will invest and divest after you invested, YOU can suffer costs because of these other investors! Unbelievable, right? In fact, many people in the industry refer to these costs as "hidden costs" because many investors are not aware of them.[5,6,7]

These costs are considered to be hidden because they are undisclosed. But these hidden costs may actually be *larger* than the mutual fund's published disclosed costs![8] That is, mutual funds might be costing you more than double what you think! Can you imagine that? Let's do some simple math. Let's say that you have $100,000 to invest. You buy a mutual fund, and you know it's going to cost you around 2% in disclosed fees, or roughly $2,000. Let's say that over the course of a year the market goes up by around 8% and so you think you're going to make $8,000 on your investment, from which you paid $2,000 in disclosed fees. This would be a $6,000 return. But, because of the undisclosed "hidden" costs, you might end up "paying" an additional $2,000, thereby reducing your total return to $4,000. So, this means that you "paid" $4,000 (i.e., $2,000 disclosed cost plus $2,000 hidden cost) to get $4,000. Hahaha. I guess this hidden cost is why some experts consider mutual funds to be a "drag on your retirement."[9] You might think that these costs are difficult to explain or understand, but really they are not. I will describe these undisclosed "hidden" costs now. But to help explain them, I want you to first consider the following two situations, which should help you to understand the costs that I will be describing shortly.

Situation A:

During a given week, let's say that a bunch of individual investors decide to invest a total of $50 million into a $500 million mutual fund. Here, the fund will take the new investors' $50 million and buy more stocks with it, and then it will become a $550 million fund.

Situation B:

During a given week, let's say that a bunch of individual investors decide to divest $50 million from a

$500 million fund. Here, the fund has to sell $50 million worth of stocks to obtain the cash to give to the divesting investors, and then it will become a $450 million fund.

Now, given the above two situations, there are three costs that YOU can personally suffer because of these other investors investing and divesting into your fund. I will try to explain each cost in turn.

1. Commissions

When a mutual fund buys additional stocks to accommodate subsequent new investors after you invested in the fund, the fund, of course, typically has to pay broker commissions. But note that this can eat away at the value of your investment and your returns![10,11] Think about it. Say that you buy a mutual fund today. Then, next month, the mutual fund receives more cash from new investors. The fund then uses this cash to buy more stocks. When the fund pays broker commissions for the stock purchases, this cost is included as part of the costs of running a mutual fund. Of course, the fund can incur the same cost when investors sell their mutual fund shares—if the fund needs to sell stocks to cash out the investor, it would typically have to pay brokerage commissions. Under this example, part of these costs comes out of the amount that you originally invested or out of the year-end distribution that is paid out to all of the funds' investors, including YOU, even though it's the other investors who are causing this cost! Let's just imagine this…. Today, you buy a fund and then you do nothing, but the fund that you own continues to pay extra brokerage commissions due to *others'* trading. How fair is this to you? Not fair at all.

Okay, that was the easiest of the three costs to explain. Now I'll explain two other subtle costs. And by the way, just because these other costs can be subtle, that doesn't mean they are trivial.

2.i Bid–ask spreads

This section is denoted "2.i" because there are two parts to this cost. Part 1, which describes the cost, is going to annoy you if you already own mutual funds. Part 2, where I explain why this cost can be particularly large for some mutual funds, is likely going to annoy you even more. By the way, don't forget that I'm just the messenger. Don't be annoyed at me!

Have you ever tried selling your used car to a car dealership? If you have, then you may be familiar with this scenario. First, you look up the estimated price of your car on the Internet (maybe you'll use Kelly Blue Book to get your price estimate). You discover that your used car is worth a decent amount of money and you become happy and start imagining ways of how you're going to spend this money. Now, let's say that you personally do not want to find a buyer for your car yourself because, after all, you're a busy person, and so, for the sake of convenience, you decide to take your car to a car dealership. At the dealership, to your shock and dismay, the car dealer offers you quite a low price for your car. You argue with the dealer that your car is worth more, but the dealer will give you his or her reasons for offering you a low price. For example, one thing that the dealer might say is, "I have to make money on this car." (And you know, this is a fair point. The dealer does need to be, and should be, compensated for his or her service because without the dealer you might not be able to find a buyer at all.) Let's say that you accept the dealer's offer. You go home feeling pretty annoyed.

Have you ever tried buying a used car at a car dealership? If you have, then I bet you felt like you got ripped off or fleeced on the price. In the least, you probably felt unsure about the price that you paid.

The stocks that most of us buy are kind of like used cars. We're buying them from other investors, through securities dealers. Like used car dealers, these securities dealers buy stocks at one price (the "bid price") and resell them at a higher price (the "ask price"). So, just like the car dealer, the ask price is typically always higher than the bid price. This "bid–ask spread" is a way that securities dealers (and used car dealers) can make their money on trades. They buy at bid prices that are lower than their resell prices.

How does all of this bid–ask spread stuff affect you, especially after you buy a mutual fund? Would you sell a $20 bill for $19.50 and buy a $20 bill for $20.50? Of course not. You'd be losing $1 on this "spread."

In similar fashion, after you buy a mutual fund, if your mutual fund continues to buy stocks at a higher ask price and sell at lower bid price, this causes the fund (and thus also YOU TOO)[12] to lose money.

This is making you annoyed, right? Grab a drink before reading further, as there's more to these "transactions" costs that I will explain.

2.ii Bid–ask spreads, Part II:
The impact of adverse selection on spreads

Got your drink in hand? Take a swig and read the following. Let me now explain how something called "adverse selection" can make bid–ask spreads even wider, and how mutual funds, in particular, can especially suffer from this adverse selection problem.[13,14]

Unlike you and me, mutual funds usually don't buy only hundreds, or thousands, or even tens of thousands of dollars' worth of stocks. Instead, when a financial institution, such as a mutual fund firm, buys and sells stocks, their transactions can be quite large. They might, and easily can, for example, buy millions of dollars' worth of Google stock. Okay, okay, I guess individuals like Bill Gates and Warren Buffet can also buy millions of dollars' worth of stock, but I am referring to you and me, not to them. And yes, I'm pretty sure that you are not Bill Gates or Warren Buffet, because they probably already know about all of the issues with mutual funds. Think about it. Do you think they own a ton of mutual funds? Hahahaha, I don't think so. But wow, that's funny. Mark Zuckerburg, Bono, Barack Obama, Mitt Romney, Oprah Winfrey, Derek Jeter, Brad Pitt, CEOs of Citigroup, McDonalds, GE, and Mark Cuban (he's the outspoken owner of the Dallas Mavericks and is on the television show, Shark Tank), and so on, investing a ton of money in mutual funds? Hahahaha. I can't stop laughing. Mark Cuban owning mutual funds, when he can afford to hire his own financial advisors? Why would he choose to "hire" a mutual fund manager when he can afford to hire the best money managers on the planet and avoid all of the problems with mutual funds? Hahahaha.

Anyway, sorry for the digression, but the point is:

Wealthy people probably do not buy archaic investments like mutual funds. And if they don't, then why should we? Don't you want to invest the way they do? In the 21st century, we all can, through a separately managed account (see SMA discussion in Chapter 8). SMAs are a straight-forward way to invest in many stocks, which was not easily doable with the technology, trading costs, and administrative costs of the past. With new technology, having your own SMA is sort of like having your very own *personal* mutual fund.

According to Wikipedia's characterization of SMAs:

> SMAs are popular with wealthier investors and their financial advisers as they are seen as exclusive, and offer investment options not available to those of more modest means.[15]

Well, that used to be the case. Like I said, with the

technology that is available today and with more firms utilizing that technology (this includes my firm!), those of us with "modest means" (this includes me!) *can* invest in SMAs (I did!). I'll discuss SMAs, in more detail, in Chapter 8 of this book.

Hey, are you skimming this book? If so, then you may have missed the paragraphs above. Read them. I think they're pretty amusing and important.

Anyway, let me get back on point. So, what's the big deal when a mutual fund buys millions of dollars of stock? Let's say a mutual fund wants to purchase 2 million shares of Cool Cars stock. The fund goes to a securities dealer to buy them, but the securities dealer may only have 500,000 shares available to sell at his or her best ask price (a "best ask price" is the lowest standby price that a dealer is ready to sell a stock). Since the fund wants to buy an additional 1.5 million shares of Cool Cars stock, it then has to pay the dealer a higher price for those shares. Why doesn't the dealer just sell all 2 million shares for the same price? There is something known as "adverse selection." It's an academic term, but the concept is really easy to understand. If you were a stock dealer, and a financial institution wants to buy tons of Cool Cars stocks from you, wouldn't you think that the financial institution might know something that you don't? Maybe Cool Cars stock is super fantastic, but only the financial institution knows this right now. After all, there are probably a lot of smart people who work at the financial institution. So, to help protect yourself from selling a great stock for a bargain, you might only let financial institutions and other investors purchase a specific amount of shares at your most competitive ask price. If they want more than this specific amount, then they have to pay a higher ask price for them. This pricing policy can protect the dealer from selling too many shares of a possibly fantastic stock at a bargain.

By the way, this also applies to mutual funds *selling* stocks too. If a mutual fund wants to sell 2 million shares of Cool Cars stock, the fund may not be able to sell them all to a securities dealer at his or her current ready-to-buy "best bid price." This means that the fund may have to sell off some of those 2 million shares at a discount.

Okay, the above is a pretty clear illustration of what adverse selection is and how it works. But you're probably still wondering what this all has to do with you. Well, imagine this. You buy a mutual fund today. And then, you do nothing. But the fund is still actively buying and selling stocks, especially given the fact that other investors are investing into the fund and divesting from the fund. Given that, this means that mutual funds can place very large orders to buy and sell stocks and that a part of their large order to buy may get filled at very high ask prices and a part of their large order to sell may be filled at very low bid prices.[16] In other words, because of mutual funds' large orders to buy and sell stock, they may experience large bid–ask spreads. I already told you how these spreads can lose you money. Well, what I'm telling you now is that these spreads can be especially large for mutual fund firms. (And, by the way, don't make the mistake of thinking that a mutual fund can get a "large quantity discount" or a good price just because they are buying lots of stocks. That'd be pretty funny. I know the price of donuts and the price of wine are cheaper when you buy them by the dozen, but you can't say to a securities dealer, "I'd like to buy a lot of IBM stock, and since I'm buying a lot, can you give me a discount or can you give me a few IBM shares for free?" Hahaha, that'd be funny. In fact, I might try that the next time I talk to a securities dealer, just for laughs.)

So, overall, bid–ask spreads can lose you money. And, therefore, you can actually be losing this money even if the mutual fund is NOT doing any of this buying or selling on your behalf! And, these spreads could be huge because of adverse selection!

Speaking of large buy and sell orders, they not only cause bid–ask spreads to widen, they can also have another adverse effect on you! Read the next section.

Warning: Reading further may annoy you even more.

3.i Price impact

This cost is kind of related to the above bid–ask spread costs, but it's also a unique cost in and of itself. Let's say that Tasty Food stock is currently priced at $20 per share. Now let's say that you want to buy a million shares of Tasty Food stock. Do you think you can buy them all at $20 per share? Based on what I wrote above, you already know that you probably cannot because of bid–ask spreads and adverse selection. But let's ignore bid–ask spreads and adverse selection for now. Let me repeat the question. Do you think you can buy a million shares of Tasty Food stock for $20 a share? Probably not. You see, when there is a large demand for something, then the price of that something usually goes up. It's not rocket science, it's logical and it's really that simple. Why are Super Bowl tickets so expensive? It is partly because there is a high demand for those tickets. Large demand can affect stock prices too.[17] If someone buys a million shares of a stock, that stock price will usually rise, simply from the large buy order in and of itself. This effect is called "price impact."

So, how does this price impact cause you to lose you money? Imagine the following. You buy a mutual fund, and then you do nothing thereafter. However, when the mutual fund buys stock, they aren't very likely to be buying a few shares of stock. Instead, they might be buying many thousands or even millions of shares of stock. Right now, let's say your mutual fund owns Banana Computer stock currently worth $80 per share. If the fund decides to buy a million more shares of Banana stock, this large demand by itself may cause Banana share price to increase. Let's say that it increases to $81/share (some of the increase is coming from the spread and some of it is coming from the price impact of the mutual fund's trade). Now, do you see what's about to happen? Your fund is going to pay $81 for an $80 stock!! Do you like paying MORE than what something is worth? Of course not. Have you ever said to anyone, "I'll pay you $21 for a $20 bill."? Of course you haven't. But that's what YOUR mutual fund will be doing. Remember, Banana stock is currently worth $80 per share. But because of the mutual fund's large buy order, it could cause the stock price to go up and the fund may end up paying, let's say, $81 per share. This extra $1 payment has to come from somewhere. From where? From all of the investors in the fund, including YOU. This specific cost to mutual fund investors is pretty well-known and is sometimes referred to as a "market impact cost," and it has been suggested that this cost is quite significant.[18]

And, of course, this price impact effect can apply to mutual funds selling stocks, too. That may also have a bad consequence to you. If your mutual fund *sells* a million shares of Banana stock, the large sale order by itself might cause Banana stock price to fall, let's say, to $79/share. Remember, Banana stocks are really worth $80/share. Do you want your mutual fund to sell Banana stocks for less than what their worth? Have you ever said to anyone, "I'll sell you a $20 bill for $19."? Of course you haven't. But the fund's large sell order, by itself, could drive the stock price down when they execute their large sale, so that it ends up paying, let's say, $79 for an $80 stock. Congratulations, I guess. Your fund now has $79 in cash instead of an $80 stock. And by the way, maybe this $79 per share is just short of the $80 per share that the fund needed to raise, and thus it has to sell more Banana stock at $79/share to cover the difference.

So, price impact can affect you negatively. The large buying and selling that mutual funds do, in and of themselves, may cause stock prices to increase and decrease.[19] Under this example, the fund buys stocks for more than what the stocks are really worth and the fund sells stock for less than what they are really worth. As I said before, this is like buying **$20** bills for **$21** *(some of the extra $1 is coming from the spread and some of it is coming from the price impact)* and selling **$20** bills for **$19** *(some of the $1 loss can be due to the spread and some of it can be due to the price impact)*. The takeaway from this discussion is simple: You may be losing money even when you do nothing.

Now, at this point, I want you to realize the following. If you owned your own personal portfolio of stocks, then it is unlikely you will be buying millions of shares of any stock. After all, you are not a large financial institution like a mutual fund with billions of dollars to invest on behalf of thousands or millions of investors. So, if you decide to buy and sell Banana stock, it will probably not affect the stock price at all. That is, you won't experience the adverse effects of price impact because your individual and relatively small trade sizes will not cause stock prices to move. In other words, you won't suffer from market impact costs.

By the way, did you notice that this section is denoted "3.i"? Uh oh, you know what that means don't you? There is another part to these costs.

3.ii Price impact, Part II

When a stock's price increases only because there is a large spike in a mutual fund's demand for that stock, the price increases can be temporary.[20] Think about it. In this example, the price change is NOT occurring for any fundamental reason. That is, the stock price is not increasing because the firm discovered a new invention or innovation, or discovered oil, or hired a great CEO. Instead, the stock price can be increasing because the mutual fund is simply buying lots of stock when new investors buy into the fund. In the real world, this can mean that eventually those stock prices will come back down to their fundamental levels.

What? Did somebody say double-whammy!?

The first whammy: The fund submits a large buy order for a stock, causing the stock price to increase, which, in turn, can lead to the fund paying more for the stock than what the stock is really worth. So, for example, the fund pays $81 for an $80 stock. Here, you lost a dollar. But, you might say, "Okay, I get it, the fund spent $81 for an $80 stock, and I realize that stinks, but at least the fund owns what is now an $81 stock." Hehehe, okay, get ready for the second whammy.

The second whammy: After the fund buys the stock, the stock price will eventually revert back to its original fundamental value, because, in our example, the fundamental value is the actual real value. So, the fund could pay $81 for an $80 stock, and after it buys the stock, the stock will eventually go back to $80. Under this example you just lost another dollar.

Wham, wham. That's the sound of you getting whacked… twice.

Proof that these hidden costs are real.

Before I conclude this chapter, let me offer the following. Whenever anyone makes an argument, he or she should always consider opposite viewpoints. So, I'd like to do that now. As I review this chapter's contents, I think the only issue that a detractor could raise is that bid–ask spreads are not as large as they used to be. This is a fair point. Are you old enough to remember when stock prices were in increments of 1/8th of a dollar? I am. Actually, this wasn't that long ago. Hahaha. How embarrassing. Our country with the most sophisticated financial system in the world was pricing stocks in 1/8ths. Whoops, I'm digressing, sorry. Anyway, today, stock prices are in increments of decimals, that is, in cents. So, in the "old days," the smallest bid–ask spread that you could possibly have is 1/8th of a dollar, but today, the spread can be much less. This means that the bid–ask spread cost that I described in Section 2.i may be minor. So, even though you could continue to suffer costs after you buy a mutual fund, these costs may be small. Umm, does this make you feel better? Wouldn't it be better if you didn't suffer any of this cost at all? And, by the way, when anyone uses the point that "today's spreads are smaller than they used to be," ask him or her about the effect that I describe in Section 2.ii, that adverse selection can make spreads wider. He or she might also say that the adverse selection effect is also smaller today because we now price stocks in decimals (i.e., in cents). I would actually dispute this point. We all know that spreads can be narrow when there are a lot of buyers and sellers (i.e., when there is a liquid market). But the scenario that I described in Section 2.ii is where there is a single large buy (or sell) order submitted by a single mutual fund. In such a scenario, the spread can of course certainly be large. But okay, okay, I don't want to get into an argument over whether adverse selection costs are big or small. We can all agree that a cost exists, and that's my main point.

By the way, I'm not done. Also ask my detractors about the effects that I described in Sections 3.i and 3.ii. Are they small today too? They might say so, arguing that markets may be more efficient today than they used to be. But, uh, at some point, the adding up of a bunch of small costs could eventually be equal to a big cost.

So, overall, I do not think my detractors have much of a case.

Finally, here's the best proof that I can give you that the costs that I describe in this chapter are both real and significant. Are you ready? Here it is. You do realize that there are many mutual funds out there that brag about their low turnovers, right?[21] Well, think about it. Why would they brag about low turnovers if the costs described in this chapter were not real? Why would they brag about low turnovers if the costs described in this chapter were small?[22] I have a point here, don't I? I love it when I can end an argument on a high note. So, when a fund is bragging about their low turnover, what they are really bragging about is that their undisclosed "hidden" costs are not that huge. Hahaha, isn't this like a thief who brags that he doesn't steal that much?

Other costs

Dang it. I wanted to end this chapter on a high

note with my last paragraph above, but I have a few other costs that I should mention. Mutual funds have expenses that other investments normally do not have. Mutual funds usually have to pay for the following[23] :

- Administrator
- Accountant
- Auditor
- Board of directors

I would imagine the above are not cheap. I guess this is part of the reason for why mutual fund fees are so high.

On to the next chapter.

Chapter 3 Endnotes:

[5] Edelen, R., Evans, R., & Kadlec, G. (2013). Shedding light on "invisible" costs: Trading costs and mutual fund performance. *Financial Analysts Journal*, 69(1). doi: 10.2469/faj.v69.n1.6. Retrieved from http://www.cfapubs.org/doi/pdf/10.2469/faj.v69.n1.6.

[6] Prior, A. (2010, March 1). The hidden costs of mutual funds. *Wall Street Journal*. Retrieved from http://online.wsj.com/articles/SB1000142405274870338290457505969095487072 2.

[7] Mahoney, P. G. (2004). Manager-investor conflicts in mutual funds. *Journal of Economic Perspectives*, 18, 161–182.

[8] Bernicke, T. A. (2011, April 4). The real cost of owning a mutual fund. *Forbes*. Retrieved from http://www.forbes.com/2011/04/04/real-cost-mutual-fund-taxes-fees-retirement-bernicke.html.

[9] Tuchman, M. (2014, February 19). A hidden way mutual funds cost you money. Forbes. Retrieved from http://www.forbes.com/sites/mitchelltuchman/2014/02/19/a-hidden-way-mutual-funds-cost-you-money/.

[10] Prior (2010).

[11] Edelen et al. (2013).

[12] Prior (2010).

[13] A basic definition of "adverse selection" is here: Adverse selection. (n.d.) Retrieved from http://en.wikipedia.org/wiki /Adverse_selection. The term is often used to explain why insurance companies charge high premiums and limit coverage. Specifically, because insurance companies are aware that high-risk individuals are the ones that specifically seek insurance, the insurance companies charge high premiums and limit coverage to them.

[14] Academic papers that describe how adverse selection affects bid–ask spreads include the following:

❖ Heflin, F., & Shaw, K. W. (2005). Trade size and informed trading: Which trades are "big"? *Journal of Financial Research*, 20, 133–163.

❖ Affleck-Graves, J., Hegde, S. P., & Miller, R. E.. (1994). Trading mechanisms and the components of the bid-ask spread. *Journal of Finance*, 49, 1471–1488.

❖ Stoll, H. R. (1978). The pricing of security dealer services: An empircal study of Nasdaq stocks. *Journal of Finance*, 33, 1153–1172.

[15] Separately managed account. (n.d.). Retrieved from http://en.wikipedia.org/ wiki/ Separately_managed_account.

[16] Market makers (finance). (n.d.). Retrieved from http://what-when-how.com/finance/ market-makers-finance.

[17] Edelen et al. (2013, pp. 7–8) describe how "price impact" impairs mutual fund returns. Some academics call it a "price pressure" effect. Ben-Rephael, A., Kandel, S., & Wohl, A. (2011). The price pressure of aggregate mutual fund flows. *Journal of Financial and Quantitative Analysis*, 46, 585–603.

An academic paper that broadly describes how large buying and selling causes this price impact effect is Harris, L., & Gurel, E. (1986). Price and volume effects associated with changes in the S&P 500 list: New. *Journal of Finance*, 41, 815–829.

[18] Prior (2010).

[19] Prior (2010).

[20] Ben-Rephael (2011, p. 14).

[21] The potential problem of high turnover in mutual funds is well known. For example, see:

❖ Cohn, L. (29 March 2010). The case for low-turnover funds. Retrieved from http://m.kiplinger.com/article/investing /T041-C009-S001-the-case-for-low-turnover-funds.html>.

❖ Barker, B. (n.d..). Turnover and cash reserves. Retrieved from http://www.fool. com/School/MutualFunds/Costs/Turnover.htm.

[22] Lenzner, R. (2013, May 30). Mutual funds biting the dust at an alarming rate. Retrieved from http://www.forbes.com/sites/robertlenzner/2013/05/30/mutual-funds-biting-the-dust-at-an-alarming-rate/.

[23] Mutual fund. (n.d.). Retrieved from http://en.wikipedia.org/wiki/Mutual_fund.

Chapter Four
Why do mutual funds underperform?

Here's a mystery. Why do mutual funds underperform? This underperformance is notoriously well-known and sometimes even joked about in the popular press,[24,25] and it is also a subject of much study in academia.[26] Truly, this is bizarre. We often hear that picking stocks is so hard to do that if you were to throw darts randomly at a list of stocks and create a portfolio consisting of these dartboard stocks, that it would do just as well as stocks picked by so-called experts. This notion is so popular that the *Wall Street Journal* even once featured a "dartboard column" where they pitted so-called expert stock pickers against randomly chosen stocks.[27] I don't remember exactly, but I think the pros beat the dartboard a little bit more than half the time. You would think, therefore, that just based on randomness, mutual funds would be known for pretty much matching the market's performance, *on average*, rather than underperforming the market. Many possible explanations have been put forth for why mutual funds underperform. Here are just four possible causes that I think are the most plausible (and, by the way, I'm ignoring mutual fund's disclosed fees, which is another obvious reason why actively managed mutual funds might not generate the same returns as the market[28]).

First, most mutual funds suffer from undisclosed "hidden" costs. These costs can eat into your returns. What's a hidden cost? Ha, you skipped Chapter 3. I caught you red-handed. Read it. The undisclosed "hidden" costs of mutual funds may be one of the primary causes of their underperformance.

Second, for mutual fund managers, their fund's performance is typically not directly linked to their compensation. Therefore, for instance, a fund manager may not be paid based upon his or her success in generated gains for investors. A fund manager can get compensated from the fees she or he charges for managing the fund, which is typically a percentage of the fund's total assets. In this scenario, a fund manager's compensation will increase when the fund increases in size, and therefore fund growth becomes one of the manager's primary goals.[29] If the fund manager sees his or her primary goal as fund growth, this is likely different from your goal, which I'm guessing is to get nice returns on your mutual fund investment. This difference in goals is known as the principal–agent problem or agency costs of mutual funds. That is, it's your money, so you're the principal, and you "hire" an agent (the mutual fund manager) to manage your money in the fund, but the two of you could have different goals. There is academic research that shows that these differing goals may contribute to fund underperformance.[30]

Third, there seems to be a lot of turnover of mutual fund managers. For example, good mutual fund managers seem to be going to hedge funds that may be willing to offer higher pay. As a result, many mutual funds may have inexperienced managers, and this might explain their underperformance. In fact, academic studies support this contention.[31] This is kind of funny because many investors might think that the value-added of investing in a mutual fund is the fund manager's investing expertise and experience, but you could lose your fund manager and his or her expertise and experience due to turnover, and the replacement manager may have neither. Further, for those funds that did well in the past, investors might buy them thinking that the fund will continue to do well in the future, BUT because of manager turnover, it's quite possible that the manager responsible for those great past returns is no longer with the fund. Finally, did you know that some funds even outsource management? Hahaha, this is funny because many people buy mutual funds because they think the mutual fund firm will manage them. But what's not funny is that for those funds that outsource their management, well,... their funds underperform.[32]

Fourth, mutual funds may be over-diversified by holding "too many" securities.[33] This "over-diversification" may be driving down the fund's ability to obtain good returns, *and* maintaining too many securities, of course, also potentially increases the size of mutual funds' undisclosed "hidden" costs. You know, this over-diversification problem of mutual funds is so significant, and really a problem all on its own, that I feel that it deserves its own chapter. So....

Chapter 4 Endnotes:

[24] Durden, T. (2013, January 5). 88% of hedge funds, 65% of mutual funds underperform market in 2012. Retrieved from http://www.zerohedge.com/news/2013-01-05/88-hedge-funds-65-mutual-funds-underperform-market-2012.

[25] Freeburn, C. (2012, September 24). 2012 banking survey: Banks go fee happy. Retrieved from http://investorplace.com/2012/09/2012-banking-survey-banks-go-fee-happy/#.U86c2_ldX0Q.

[26] Fama, E. F., & French, K. R.. (2010). Luck versus skill in the cross-section of mutual fund returns. *Journal of Finance*, 65, 1915–1947.

[27] Ensign, R. L. (2013, April 14). Darts top readers in final print contest. *Wall Street Journal*. Retrieved from http://online.wsj.com/ news/articles/10001424127887324 504704578410864000872642.

[28] See the second point raised in this article: Finger, R. (2013, April 15). Five reasons your mutual fund probably underperforms the market. Retrieved from http://www.forbes.com/sites/richardfinger/2013/04/15/five-reasons-your-mutual-fund-probably-underperforms-the-market.

[29] Cohen, R., Polk, C. &, Silli, B. (2010, March 15). Best ideas. SSRN working paper, p. 2.

[30] Mahoney (2004, p. 164).

[31] Golec, J. H. (1996). The effects of mutual fund managers' characteristics on their portfolio performance, risk and fees. *Financial Services Review*, 5, 133–147.

[32] Chen, J., Hong, H., Jiang, W., & Kubik, J. (2013). Outsourcing mutual fund management: Firm boundaries, incentives, and performance. *Journal of Finance*, 68, 523–558.

[33] Haigney, A. (2012, March 13). The curse of over-diversification. Retrieved from http://www.businessinsider.com/the-curse-of-over-diversification-2012-3

Chapter Five
Mutual funds can over-diversify

Warning—even though this is a really important chapter, it is also a really long chapter (it even has a subchapter). If you read the whole chapter, I'll give you a reward for your effort at the end of the chapter (don't cheat by jumping to the end), but first I'll provide you with the "Cliff Notes" version of the points that I am going to make in this long chapter:

• Portfolio diversification can be great.

• But analysis shows that you can achieve the benefits of portfolio diversification with only around 25 to 30 stocks (maybe up to 70 if you want to be globally diversified).

• Many mutual funds can hold hundreds of stocks, which suggests that some stocks may just be fillers, that is, not the fund manager's favorite stocks.

• Mutual funds also may hold hundreds of stocks because of regulations and basic flaws in the mutual fund industry structure, incentives, and goals. These incentives and goals may not fully align with the goals of mutual fund investors.

• As a result of the above, it can cause mutual funds to underperform benchmarks.

• Note also that when a fund holds hundreds more stocks, then it can suffer more from mutual fund's undisclosed "hidden" costs.

Before reading this chapter, please do the following: Get rid of the notion that being over-diversified may not be a bad thing! You might be thinking, "Eh, what's wrong with being too safe?" Well, there is something very wrong with it if you are paying a lot for an unnecessary level of safety. Let me put it this way. If you don't want to get sick, then you can always live in a bubble. Are you willing to live in a bubble? Even though it'd be a great way to reduce risk, you're likely not willing to make that excessive sacrifice. That is, it can actually be a bad thing to be overly safe. An issue with mutual funds is that if they are overly safe then they may be sacrificing your returns while also incurring large undisclosed "hidden" costs. Read on.

To first understand the problem of over-diversification, it'd be useful if we can do a quick review of diversification in general. Let me do that now.

Diversification 101

Portfolio diversification, in and of itself, can be a great thing, but only if it follows sound risk/reward principles. For example, if a portfolio is broadly diversified across different asset *types*, then it may lead to a nice risk/reward tradeoff. But a nice risk/reward tradeoff cannot always be achieved by simply holding *many* assets. Let me illustrate what I mean by all of this by starting off with the following example. (And, by the way, don't skip the math illustration below. It's easy to follow. Ignore those people who say that portfolio mathematics is difficult to understand. It's NOT!)

Let's say that you have a portfolio containing only two stocks, stock ABC and stock XYZ (I know these are uncreative made-up stock names, sorry), and you own an equal dollar amount of each stock in your portfolio. And let's say there are only two possible future outcomes, Outcome 1 and Outcome 2, and that each outcome has a 50% chance of occurring. So, given the above simple situation, let's say that there are three possible scenarios:

Scenario 1:

	ABC Stock Returns	XYZ Stock Returns	Portfolio Returns
Outcome 1	12%	8%	10%
Outcome 2	6%	4%	5%
Expected Return	9%	6%	**7.5%**

Scenario 2:

	ABC Stock Returns	XYZ Stock Returns	Portfolio Returns
Outcome 1	12%	6%	9%
Outcome 2	6%	6%	6%
Expected Return	9%	6%	**7.5%**

Scenario 3:

	ABC Stock Returns	XYZ Stock Returns	Portfolio Returns
Outcome 1	12%	4%	8%
Outcome 2	6%	8%	7%
Expected Return	9%	6%	**7.5%**

Now, pay attention. We're going to do a little Finance 101. In Scenario 1, if Outcome 1 occurs in the future, then your portfolio will generate a 10% return, since one stock in your portfolio got a 12% return and the other stock got an 8% return. If Outcome 2 occurs in the future, then your portfolio will generate a 5% return. Now, since there is a 50% chance of Outcome 1 occurring and a 50% percent chance of Outcome 2 occurring, then this means that the *average expected* return on your portfolio is 7.5%, since this is just the simple average of a 10% portfolio return (in Outcome 1) and a 5% portfolio return (in Outcome 2). Simple to follow, right? Scenario 2 is the same as scenario 1, except XYZ returns are the same 6% in both outcomes.

However, Scenario 3 is different from the other scenarios. In Scenario 3, the stocks that are picked will move in opposite directions from each other. Therefore, the XYZ stock returns almost always move in the opposite direction of ABC stock returns. That is, when ABC stock has "good" large returns, then XYZ stocks have "bad" small returns.

Now, check this out. The expected portfolio returns of all three scenarios are an identical 7.5%. But which scenario has the *safest* portfolio? Of course, it's the one in Scenario 3. You expect a 7.5% portfolio return, but the worst that can happen is that you get a 7% return. Hey, that's not risky at all! The standard deviation of this portfolio is only 0.5%.

Which is the *riskiest* portfolio? Of course, it's the one in Scenario 1. You again expect a 7.5% portfolio return, but this time the worst that can happen is that you only get a 5% return. Whoa, this is risky. The standard deviation of this portfolio is 2.5%.

Why is Scenario 3 safest? It's actually easy to see. It's because the returns of ABC stock and XYZ stock are negatively correlated. That is, when one stock has bad returns, the other stock has good returns. In fact, in Scenario 3, no matter which outcome occurs, you always have one stock giving you good returns.

Overall, there are a two amazing things about this simple numerical example. First, it shows that you can reduce risk, WITHOUT sacrificing returns. There's a popular saying, "less risk, less return." Well, in my example, you can reduce risk *without* sacrificing returns. This is why proper portfolio diversification can be amazing. If you had to sacrifice returns to obtain risk reduction, we academics and industry professionals wouldn't be tooting the horn of diversification. However, you may be one of those people who see "the glass as half-empty" and contend that Scenario 3 is not good because it will *always* have a stock with "bad" returns. Here is my response to you: What sacrifice are you making being in Scenario 3, since *all* of portfolios in the above three scenarios are giving you the *same* expected returns? If the portfolio in Scenario 3 gives you the same return as the portfolios in the other scenarios, but with the lowest risk, you're not making any sacrifice at all!

With regard to the second amazing thing about my simple example, let's look at the three scenarios again, and let's look closely at the risks of each stock and also of the portfolios. For your convenience, I've replicated the tables above, but this time I replaced expected returns with standard deviations.

Scenario 1: You have two risky stocks

	ABC Stock Returns	XYZ Stock Returns	Portfolio Returns
Outcome 1	12%	8%	10%
Outcome 2	6%	4%	5%
Standard Deviation	3%	2%	**2.5%**

Scenario 2: You have one risky stock and one safe stock

	ABC Stock Returns	XYZ Stock Returns	Portfolio Returns
Outcome 1	12%	6%	9%
Outcome 2	6%	6%	6%
Standard Deviation	3%	0%	**1.5%**

Scenario 3: You have two risky stocks

	ABC Stock Returns	XYZ Stock Returns	Portfolio Returns
Outcome 1	12%	4%	8%
Outcome 2	6%	8%	7%
Standard Deviation	3%	2%	**0.5%**

By focusing on the standard deviations, you can see the second amazing thing about my simple example. The table above shows that it is possible to own two risky stocks (this occurs in Scenario 3) and have a safer portfolio than owning one risky stock and one safe stock (this occurs in Scenario 2)!! Look at Scenario 3. Wow, those two stocks are risky. ABC stock has a standard deviation of 3%, while XYZ stock has a standard deviation of 2%. I look upon these as pretty large standard deviations, especially relative to each of their individual expected returns. Now look at Scenario 2. Here, ABC stock is as risky as it is in Scenario 3. However, XYZ stock has a standard deviation of 0% and so it has NO risk. But look at the portfolio standard deviations of Scenarios 2 and 3. The deviation is lower in Scenario 3, even though it contains two risky stocks! Ta da! Two risky stocks may sometimes be safer than one risky stock and one safe stock. Counter-intuitive, right? But it's true! But, of course, sometimes a portfolio with two risky stocks can make a risky portfolio... duh. This is what happens in Scenario 1. That portfolio has two risky stocks, and that portfolio is the riskiest of the three scenarios. So again, portfolio diversification can be amazing, but as long as you know how to do it, or have someone who does help you.

For the most part, Harry Markowitz is credited with the above discoveries. He's the one that suggested that we should look at how stocks are correlated to one another.[34]

And that the benefit of portfolio diversification comes from stocks that are not highly positively correlated with each other. And for this discovery, he won the Nobel Prize in Economics in 1990.[35]

So, this is what I believe good money managers should try to do. They should try to pick stocks with low or negative correlations with each other to help minimize risk WITHOUT sacrificing returns. This approach can be achieved by a qualified finance professional who can understand these principles. (You know how in those exciting car commercials, where professional drivers push cars to their limits, there is always the caption "do not try this at home, these are professional drivers"? Well, I guess I could say the same thing about replicating Scenario 3. "Do not try this at home." I believe that Scenario 3 is a strategy that is best left to professional money managers.)

Now let's make a realistic extension to my simple made-up numerical example. Instead of only two stocks and only two possible outcomes, let's think about stock returns in the real world. In my simple example, I assumed that I knew what stock ABC's and stock XYZ's returns would be in the future under each of the three scenarios. Of course, in real life, we cannot predict stock returns this accurately. So, even when we think stock returns will be negatively correlated or uncorrelated with one another, we could end up being wrong. A second important point about the real-world is that there will always be some risk that we cannot eliminate. For example, if we discover a firm's executives have been lying about the firm's earnings, disclosure of this fact may cause the firm's stock to take a nosedive. Or, if a star CEO gets hit by a car and dies, then his firm's stock might take a free-fall. Obviously, we can never reliably predict these "random" events. We normally call this risk of random occurrences "idiosyncratic risk."[36] Because of these risks, (1) returns can be hard to predict, and (2) returns can be affected by randomness. Do you think that holding a portfolio of only two stocks is sufficient diversification to cover this risk? Probably not. And if you agree with me that you are more likely to get the benefit of portfolio diversification if you hold more than two stocks, the question is how many more stocks do you need to hold? I'll talk about this next, and I'll show that academic research shows that you don't need to hold hundreds of stocks and why owning too many stocks would be over-diversification, and why that can be harmful (and, yes, I'll soon talk about that as well).

How many stocks are needed to have a diversified portfolio?

How many stocks should you hold in your portfolio?

Academic research has even proposed that the full benefits of diversification can be achieved with as low as 10 stocks,[37] but some academics have proposed that 30 stocks are needed.[38]

Academic research says you only need to hold around 25 to 30 stocks to achieve the benefits of domestic portfolio diversification.[39] Table 1 shows the expected standard deviation of annual returns of portfolios with different numbers of stocks.[40] As shown in the table, it indicates that if you hold over 30 stocks, the benefits of diversification increase trivially as compared to holding hundreds of stocks.

Table 1:

Number of Stocks	Standard Deviation
1	49.236
2	37.358
4	29.687
6	26.643
8	24.983
10	23.932
12	23.204
14	22.670
16	22.261
18	21.939
20	21.677
25	21.196
30	20.870
35	20.634
40	20.456
45	20.316
50	20.203
75	19.860
100	19.686
200	19.423
300	19.336
400	19.292
450	19.277
500	19.265
600	19.247
700	19.233
800	19.224
900	19.217
1000	19.211
Infinity	19.158

Hmmm, this table is kind of annoying to look at. Let me convert it into a figure. And besides, I like pictures. See Figure 1:

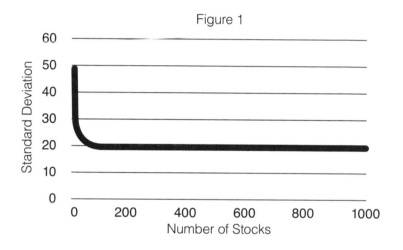

In Figure 1, the number of stocks in the portfolio is on the horizontal axis and the expected standard deviation of the portfolio is on the vertical axis. As you can see from the figure, as the portfolio contains more stocks, the risk goes down. But do you see how there's almost no difference in risk between holding 100 stocks and holding 1,000 stocks? Now, let me just show the standard deviation of a portfolio for only up to 100 stocks. See Figure 2:

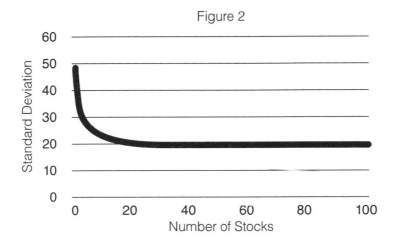

Figure 2

Figure 2 is really helpful because we can now see more precisely that the benefits of risk reduction provided by adding more stocks is pretty trivial after you already have 30 stocks. Thirty stocks, that's it![41]

Now, you probably want to know how these standard deviations were calculated. Because, after all, you may feel like you don't know who to trust, since I've been telling you that you should be skeptical of mutual funds. I have to admit that the math used to derive the standard deviations in these tables and figures is kind of complicated, so let me show you a simple and very transparent illustration that helps demonstrate that holding more than 30 may be unnecessary.

Why don't you need hundreds of stocks to be diversified?

Now, don't forget my previous numerical portfolio diversification example with Scenarios 1, 2, and 3. Remember? I was able to create a really safe portfolio with only two stocks, stocks ABC and XYZ. But that was an overly simplified example. In reality, as I previously mentioned, returns can be hard to predict, especially given idiosyncratic risk.

Now, before we go any further, let's clarify one thing. Many people in the finance and investments industry like to refer to idiosyncratic risk as the "shit happens" risk. On the one hand, I have to admit that this is a good way to describe randomness, but, on the other hand, it suggests that all random occurrences are bad, and of course this isn't necessarily the case. Just the other day when I picked up my carry-out order from my favorite Vietnamese restaurant, the restaurant was about to close and another customer had not shown up to pick up his order. So, the restaurant just let me have his carry-out order for free. That was lucky and random. And not only that, the free food that I got was something that I liked, even though I'm kind of a picky eater. Now that was really lucky and, again, random. And, on my way home, I found a thousand dollar bill! Okay, that last part didn't happen, but if it had, that also would have been a random occurrence. And all of these random occurrences can be considered good outcomes for the person that was benefitted. Companies can also experience random good luck. For example, a company could accidentally discover a cure for erectile dysfunction (true story, as Pfizer wasn't trying to find a cure for erectile dysfunction when they discovered Viagra),[42] or a company could accidentally discover Post-it notes (another true story).[43]

Now, given that a random occurrence can be either a good thing or a bad thing and given that randomness can imply a 50–50 chance that a random outcome will be good or bad, note the following. Let's say you own only two stocks and something random happens to both firms of those stocks. In this case, there is a 25% chance that both firms will experience bad luck.[44] Yikes, that's risky!

Now let's say that you own 30 stocks. And let's also say that something random happens to all of the firms of those 30 stocks. Here, there is only a 0.00000009% chance that all firms will experience bad luck.[45] Wow, that is some HUGE risk reduction! When you go from having two stocks to 30 stocks, you go from a large 25% chance that of all of your stocks will experience bad luck to a minuscule 0.00000009% chance that all of your stocks will experience bad luck. How this happens is not hard to understand. When you own 30 stocks, it's simply more likely that you will experience around an equal amount of good luck and bad luck. We have a saying for this phenomenon, which is "it'll all come out in the wash." For example...

> *Me: "Darn, I forgot my wallet. Can you pay for our lunch?"*
>
> *My friend: "Sure. No problem."*
>
> *Me: "I promise that I'll pay you back."*
>
> *My friend: "Don't worry about it. It'll all come out in the wash."*

What my friend is saying is that he and I will go out to eat many times in our lives and even though most of the time neither one of us will forget our wallets, sometimes he may randomly forget his wallet and I have to pay for both of us and sometimes I may randomly forget my wallet and he has to pay for both of us. Eventually, neither one of us is likely to have paid more than the other. Of course, this kind of eventual canceling out can only happen if we go out to eat a bunch of times. The same kind of canceling out can happen when you own a bunch of stocks, such as 30 stocks. Most of the time, random things may not happen. But when random things do occur, it's okay if you own enough stocks such that the bad luck occurrences and good luck occurrences cancel out.

However, despite my claim that significant risk reduction can be achieved with only 25 to 30 stocks, I cannot think of any mutual fund that only has this many stocks in it. Instead, they may hold *hundreds* of stocks.[46] To me, this is somewhat perplexing. I admit that I could understand it if a mutual fund held up to 70 stocks if it is globally diversified.[47] But given that many mutual funds in fact actually focus on narrow investment styles, such as large cap, value, growth, and so on, I would think that most mutual funds would actually hold *fewer* than 30 stocks. After all, if your focus is narrow, then it can be easier to be diversified within that narrow focus (e.g., for a large cap fund, they don't need to hold small cap stocks).

But mutual funds, even those focused on a specific investment style, can often hold hundreds of stocks. Now, let me ask you the following question. Do you think that a mutual fund manager can identify hundreds of great stocks? If so, then what's your definition of "great?" By definition, a great stock has to be one that is better than the majority of other stocks. So, if a mutual fund has hundreds of stocks in it, then it probably contains some great stocks, but also some stocks that are merely "fillers." These filler stocks may be the cause of mutual fund underperformance.[48] Without these filler stocks, shouldn't a mutual fund that only contains great stocks do well? If the answer is "yes," then question is, why do mutual funds hold so many stocks? In other words, why do they *over-diversify?* I will outline a few possible reasons below.

Why do mutual funds over-diversify?

There are several possible reasons why mutual funds over-diversify. First, mutual fund managers who only hold 25 stocks in their funds may feel limited in their ability to charge high fees. After all, investors might wonder why it's so expensive to manage 25 stocks. So, fund managers may hold many more stocks to help justify their high fees.[49]

Second, there are regulations that prevent mutual fund managers from being heavily concentrated in a few stocks.[50] So, to help make sure they are compliant with regulations, mutual fund managers may hold hundreds of stocks just to make it abundantly clear that they are not heavily concentrated in a few stocks. The Investment Company Institute also recognizes this tendency. From their handbook:

> If a fund elects to be diversified, the Investment Company Act requires that, with respect to at least 75 percent of the portfolio, no more than

5 percent may be invested in the securities of any one issuer and no investment may represent more than 10 percent of the outstanding voting securities of any issuer.... In practice, most funds that elect to be diversified are much more highly diversified than they need to be to meet these two tests.[51]

Third, if a mutual fund does well, then you as an investor are probably happy but the fund manager doesn't directly benefit much from the outperformance, but if the fund does poorly then the fund manager might get fired by his or her mutual fund firm.[52] When mutual fund managers consider these two divergent outcomes, they may feel it is better to prevent the latter rather than to go for the former. To be honest, I wouldn't blame them for behaving this way. I think you and I might behave similarly. We want to keep our jobs.

Fourth, mutual fund managers may be overly fixated on driving down risk to improve their Morningstar rating.[53] In general, mutual fund managers want to obtain four-star and five-star ratings from Morningstar, which is a famous research firm that evaluates and rates mutual funds.[54] If a mutual fund can obtain a high rating from Morningstar, then they may be able to attract flow (i.e., investors' money). And don't forget from Chapter 4 that mutual fund managers want flow, as this is how they can make more money. One of the most important criteria to obtain a four-star or five-star rating is to have a high Sharpe ratio, which is simply a ratio of the fund's excess returns to its risk (I will describe Sharpe ratios in detail later, and I will also describe the fallacy of Sharpe ratios). So, to help obtain a high Sharpe ratio, a fund manager could either try to find stocks with high future returns or try to reduce risk. As you can imagine, the latter is much easier to do than the former. Think about it. If I told you that your life depended on either buying stocks with high future returns or buying stocks to minimize risk, then you would obviously do the latter because all you would need to do is simply buy hundreds of stocks. Guess what? This may be what mutual fund managers do. However, overemphasis on improving return/risk ratios by driving down risk can lead to over-diversification, which I explained earlier, and may be unnecessary. But, while it may be unnecessary to be over-diversified, is it a bad thing? I'm glad that you asked....

Why over-diversification can be a bad thing

Okay, so now that we know that holding hundreds of securities may be unnecessary, you might be thinking to yourself, "Okay, I get it, being overly diversified may be unnecessary, but so what?" I have three points to make here. The first you probably already see coming. By being too fixated on reducing risk, you may be foregoing nice returns. In a supplementary Chapter 5a, I illustrate that portfolios with high Morningstar ratings (due to high Sharpe ratios) could be delivering inferior returns, while the risk-reduction benefits of having high Sharpe ratios can reduce returns.

The second point is somewhat related to the first point, but it is also a unique point in and of itself. When mutual funds add many stocks to their portfolio only to drive down idiosyncratic risk to raise their Sharpe ratios, this can mean that the few great stocks that the fund owns will get watered down. That is, given that fund managers are supposed to be investments experts, they may probably know of a handful of great stocks with promising superior returns, but they may purposely water down those returns by adding lots of "filler" stocks to their portfolio. This overfixation on Morningstar ratings and Sharpe ratios may mean that fund managers are diluting the nice returns being generated by their good stock picks! As discussed below, this has already been proven....

Mutual fund managers' "best ideas"
can get watered down

In a study by professors at Harvard and the London School of Economics, the authors find that fund managers' best stock picks (i.e., their "best ideas") outperformed benchmarks by about 1% to 4% per quarter.[55] I read the paper. It is thoroughly well executed. I believe the results. How did the researchers know which stocks were the fund manager's favorites? Simple: They identified the stocks in the managers' portfolios with the highest representation in the fund. So, if fund managers know how to pick good stocks, then why don't mutual funds outperform benchmarks? The authors conclude that fund managers fill out their portfolios with filler stocks, for reasons similar to those that I just described. By the way, this study was independently verified by a professor at the University of Toronto.[56] I read that paper too. These papers and their findings make me wish that I could buy a portfolio that only contained fund managers' *best ideas*. (Hmmm, I bet you can guess that my firm offers just such a portfolio….).

And it's not just academics who know that too many stocks may "spoil the broth." Here's a nice snippet from Investopedia:

> Dilution – It's possible to have too much diversification. Because funds have small holdings in so many different companies, high returns from a few investments often don't make much difference on the overall return. Dilution is also the result of a successful fund getting too big. When money pours into funds that have had strong success, the manager often has trouble finding a good investment for all the new money.[57]

A nice thing about the Investopedia quote is that it also describes how over-diversification can be caused by a fund getting too big. This, too, has been supported by academic research. For example, one study states, "We first document that fund returns, both before and after fees and expenses, decline with lagged fund size, even after accounting for various performance benchmarks."[58]

So, size can matter. It seems that funds should not have too many stocks and that they should not be too big. They can water down returns.

Wait, wasn't there a third reason why over-diversification can be a bad thing?

Recall that I said there are three reasons why over-diversification is potentially bad. The third reason is simply that if a mutual fund maintains many securities in their portfolio, it potentially causes the undisclosed "hidden" costs of mutual funds to go up. With each additional security that gets added to the mutual fund, which potentially increases both the number of the fund's holdings and the fund's size, your fund likely pays more commissions and can suffer more from bid–ask spreads and price impact.

Reward

This chapter was so long that you deserve a reward for getting through it, but, first, here are the main takeaways of this chapter:

- Portfolio diversification can be great.
- Analysis shows that you only need around 25 to 30 stocks to achieve the full benefits of domestic stock portfolio diversification.[59]
- But mutual funds still may hold hundreds of stocks because of regulations and flaws in the mutual fund structure.
- As a result of the above, it seems to cause mutual funds to underperform benchmarks.
- Also when a fund holds hundreds more stocks, then it can suffer more from the mutual fund's undisclosed "hidden" costs.

And now here's the reward that I promised you for reading this entire long chapter (and, by the way, you can have the reward even if you skipped to the end; shhh, this is between you and me). If you are swayed by my points, then you may want to find out how your mutual funds stack up. And so here's what I did: I prepared a "Mutual Fund Stress Test," and my firm will provide it to you. Isn't this a nice reward? To learn how you can get your own Mutual Fund Stress Test, see Chapter 9.

The next chapter is sort of like an appendix to Chapter 5. It provides an in-depth discussion on why Sharpe ratios may be a flawed way to evaluate portfolios. You should read it because many investors, including so-called sophisticated institutional investors, rely heavily on Sharpe ratios to help evaluate mutual funds. But I think this emphasis placed on Sharpe ratios is highly misplaced.

Chapter 5 Endnotes:

[34] Markowitz, H. M. (1959). *Portfolio selection: Efficient diversification of investments.* New Haven, CT: Cowles Foundation for Research in Economics at Yale University.

[35] Nobel Prize in Economics. (n.d.). Retrieved from http://simple.wikipedia.org/wiki/Nobel_Prize_in_Economics.

[36] Idiosyncratic risk. (n.d.). Retrieved from http://www.investopedia.com/ terms/i/idiosyncraticrisk.asp.

[37] Evans, J. L., & Archer, S. H. (1968). Diversification and the reduction of despersion: An empirical analysis. *Journal of Finance*, 23, 761–767.

[38] Statman, M. (1987). How many stocks make a diversified portfolio? *Journal of Financial and Quantitative Analysis*, 22, 353–363.

[39] Elton, E. J., Gruber, M. J., Brown, S. J., & Goetzmann, W. N. (2010). *Modern portfolio theory and investment analysis.* 8th ed. Hoboken, NJ: Wiley.

[40] Statman (1987, pp. 353–363).

[41] Elton et al. (2010, pp. 353–363).

[42] Jay, E. (2010, January 20). Viagra and other drugs discovered by accident. Retrieved from http://news.bbc.co.uk/2/hi /health/8466118.stm.

[43] Editors of Publications International, Ltd. (2007, September 19). 9 things invented or discovered by accident. Retrieved from http://science.howstuffworks.com/innovation/scientific-experiments/9-things-invented-or-discovered-by-accident.htm.

[44] The way that I estimated the 25% probability is as follows: $0.50n = 0.25$ when $n = 2$ stocks. This estimation is based on the assumption that the probability of good luck versus bad luck is 50% each and that causes of bad luck and good luck are independently and identically distributed. You know, here's a better way to explain it. It's like flipping a coin twice. There's a 25% chance that I'll get two heads and a 25% chance that I'll get two tails. There's a 50% chance that I'll get one head and one tail, because either the first flip can be a head and second flip is a tail (25% chance) or the first flip can be a tail and the second flip is a head (25% chance).

[45] $0.50n = 0.00000009\%$ when $n = 30$ stocks.

[46] Cohen et al. (2010).

[47] Professor Solnik states that an American investor holding 20 stocks can reduce his or her risk by another 3% if he or she held another 50 stocks from around the world (p. 48). See Solnik, B. H. (1995). Why not diversify internationally rather than domestically? *Financial Analysts Journal*, 51, 89–94.

[48] Cohen et al. (2010, p. 2).

[49] Cohen et al. (2010).

[50] Roet, M. J. (1991). Political elements in the creation of a mutual fund industry. *University of Pennsylvania Law Review*, 139, 1469-1511.

[51] Quoted text is from Investment Company Institute. (2014). 2014 investment company fact book. Retrieved from http://www.icifactbook.org/index.html.

[52] Lippert, R. L. (1996). Agency conflicts, managerial compensation, and firm variance. *Journal of Financial and Strategic Decisions*, 9, 39-47.

[53] Bhardwaj, S. (2012, March 5). Mutual fund ratios: Sharpe and Treynor. Retrieved from http://articles.economictimes.indiatimes.com/2012-03-05/news/31124018_1_treynor-ratio-risk-adjusted-sharpe-ratio.

[54] Cohen et al. (2010).

[55] Cohen et al. (2010).

[56] Pomorski, L. (2009). Acting on the most valuable information: "Best idea" trades of mutual fund managers.. Working paper, University of Toronto.

[57] Quoted text is from Investopedia: Mutual fund. (n.d.). Retrieved from http://www.investope dia.com /terms/m/mutualfund.asp.

[58] Chen, J., Hong, H., Huang, M., & Kubik, J. D. (2004). Does fund size erode mutual fund performance? The role of liquidity and organization. *American Economic Review*, 94, 1276–1302.

[59] Elton et al. (2010, pp. 353–363).

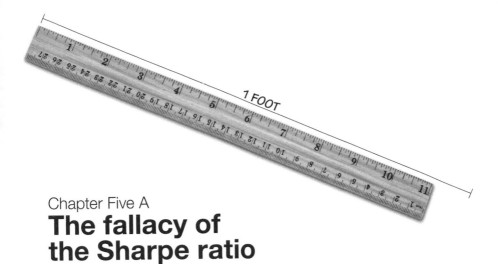

Chapter Five A
The fallacy of
the Sharpe ratio

Many investors, along with Morningstar, seem to rely heavily on Sharpe ratios to help evaluate portfolios. So you might want to understand why I think this attention to Sharpe ratios is ill-advised.[60] If not, then you can skip Chapter 5a, but I think the remaining chapters, especially Chapters 7 and 8, are really important.

Here is the usual measure of the Sharpe ratio:

(Portfolio return − risk-free return) / standard deviation of portfolio return.[61]

The numerator is the excess (or extra) return that a portfolio provides beyond the return on a risk-free investment. Usually, we tend to think of Treasury bills, notes, and bonds as a risk-free investment. The denominator is simply a measure of risk. We tend to think that return volatility is a good way to measure investment risk. That is, you might expect a 15% excess return, but if the returns can vary by a lot, then that's considered risky. The formula is not complicated. Overall, the Sharpe ratio simply reports the tradeoff between risk and return. But that is all that it is! Nothing more, nothing less. Therefore, the Sharpe ratio is only primarily useful when two portfolios have (1) the same returns but different risk or (2) the same risk but different returns. Let me demonstrate with a simple illustration.

Let's say that Portfolio A and Portfolio B have the same 10% average annual excess return from the past three years but experienced different risks. Let's say Portfolio A's past three-year annual returns had a standard deviation of 7% while Portfolio B's past three-year annual returns had a standard deviation of 8%.

So...

Portfolio A's Sharpe ratio = 1.43 (i.e., 10%/7%)

Portfolio B's Sharpe ratio = 1.25 (i.e., 10%/8%)

Portfolio A has a higher Sharpe ratio than Portfolio B. And, clearly, Portfolio A is better than Portfolio B. Portfolio A delivers the same excess return as Portfolio B, but with less volatility (i.e., less risk).

Now let's say that Portfolio A and Portfolio B have the same 7% risk but different excess returns (10% vs. 11%). So...

Portfolio A's Sharpe ratio = 1.43 (i.e., 10%/7%)

Portfolio B's Sharpe ratio = 1.57 (i.e., 11%/7%)

This time Portfolio B has a higher Sharpe ratio than Portfolio A. And, clearly, Portfolio B is better than Portfolio A. Portfolio B delivers more returns than Portfolio A but with the same risk exposure.

But, in real life, two portfolios are unlikely to have the exact same excess returns or the exact same risk. As such, Sharpe ratios often cannot tell you which portfolios are obviously better. For example, let's say that Portfolio A has 11% average annual excess returns and 8% risk, while Portfolio B has 10% average annual excess returns and 7% risk. This means...

Portfolio A's Sharpe ratio = 1.38 (i.e., 11%/8%)

Portfolio B's Sharpe ratio = 1.43 (i.e., 10%/7%)

Here, Portfolio B has a higher Sharpe ratio than Portfolio A. But can you really tell me that Portfolio B is obviously the better portfolio? For me personally, I'd go for Portfolio A. I'm willing to take on a little extra risk for the extra return.

Here's more proof that Portfolio A above is better than Portfolio B. By the way, you can skip this illustration if you want to, but what I'm about to show you is pretty cool.

For both portfolios, let's pretend we start with $1 million. To make this really easy, let's also pretend, from now on, that the risk-free return is 0% (we can get away with this for two reasons: First, Treasury rates currently are close to 0%,[62] and, second, the risk-free rate is the same for all portfolios, so it's sort of pointless to deduct the same return from portfolios when comparing portfolios). For Portfolio A, at 11% annual returns, after one year you'll have $1.11 million. After the second year, you'll have 11% more for a total of $1.23 million (i.e., $1.11 million times 1.11). After four years, you'll end up with $1.518 million. For Portfolio B, at 10% annual returns, after four years, you'll end up with only $1.464 million. I put these numbers in Table 1.

Table 1:

	Portfolio A	Portfolio B
Today	1	1
1 year later	1.110	1.100
2 years later	1.232	1.210
3 years later	1.368	1.331
4 years later	1.518	1.464

So, obviously, in this example you'll end up with more money with Portfolio A. This part, of course, you already know. The issue that we need to address is the fact that Portfolio A has more risk. Portfolio A's standard deviation is 8% as opposed to Portfolio B, which has a lower standard deviation of only 7%. To incorporate this risk difference between the two portfolios, here's what I will do. For Portfolio A, in the first year and third year, I will use a 19% return, and in the second year and fourth year, I will use a 3% return. Why will I do this? Well, when you take the four returns, 19%, 3%, 19%, and 3%, the average is 11% and the standard deviation is 8%. Don't forget that Portfolio A has a return of 11% and a risk of 8%. For Portfolio B, in the first year and third year, I will use a 17% return, and in the second year and fourth year, I will use a 3% return. The average of 17%, 3%, 17%, and 3% is 10%, and its standard deviation is 7%. Don't forget that Portfolio B has a return of 10% and a risk of 7%. To see what happens, let's look at the results below in Table 2.

Table 2:

	Portfolio A	Portfolio B
Today	1.000	1.000
1 year later	1.190	1.170
2 years later	1.226	1.205
3 years later	1.459	1.410
4 years later	1.502	1.452

There are two interesting observations from Table 2. First, we see that both portfolios experience lower values after four years when compared to Table 1. That is, in Table 1, Portfolios A and B will be worth $1.518 million and $1.464 million, respectively. In Table 2, Portfolios A and B will only be worth $1.502 million and $1.452 million, respectively. This is not surprising. Volatile returns will bring down the future value of your portfolios. This can be one of the adverse effects of risk.

The second interesting observation from Table 2 is really the amazing one.... You still end up with more money with Portfolio A, despite its higher risk! Sure, the returns fluctuate more in Portfolio A than in Portfolio B, but do you really care?

At this point, the only thing that I can think of that might still make you think that Portfolio B is better is than Portfolio A is that Portfolio A has a higher probability of having a downward movement than Portfolio B, because, after all, Portfolio A has a higher standard deviation than Portfolio B. Okay, that's a damn good point. But, err,... this is kind of awkward,... you're point is not valid. Sorry about that. Here, I'll show you. Let's say Portfolio A has a negative return of -2% in year 4. And, let's say Portfolio B never experiences a negative return. This is your point, right? That Portfolio A is more likely to experience a downturn than Portfolio B, given the fact that Portfolio A has a higher standard deviation. So, let's see what happens. And, by the way, to make sure that Portfolio A still maintains a standard deviation of 8% and an average return of 11%, I'll use the following four returns: 13%, 20%, 13%, and -2% (in fact, the standard deviation of these four returns is actually 8.03%, which is larger than 8%, which should, I suppose, help your point even more). For Portfolio B, I will keep its returns the same as in Table 2. The new Portfolio A results are below, in Table 3.

Table 3:

	Portfolio A	Portfolio B
Today	1.000	1.000
1 year later	1.130	1.170
2 years later	1.356	1.205
3 years later	1.532	1.410
4 years later	1.502	1.452

You can see from Table 3 the loss that Portfolio A experiences in year 4. It goes from a $1.532 million portfolio to a $1.502 million portfolio. The portfolio loses $30,000. I have to admit: That's a lot of money. But who cares?! In the end, Portfolio A gives you more money than Portfolio B, even though Portfolio A experiences a loss while Portfolio B never experiences a loss. The reason why Portfolio A does better is simple: It has higher returns,… duh!

By the way, an additional nice point that can be made from Table 3 is that there will be times when a riskier portfolio can lose you money, but, overall, losing some money on a great portfolio will often be worth it. For example, would you rather be given a million dollars and then lose 10% of it, or would you rather be given a hundred dollars and then lose none of it? Obviously, you prefer the former, even though there can be a loss to what you're given. So, you just have to keep these risks in perspective. Here, let me help illustrate with a picture, because, after all, a picture is supposedly worth a thousand words.

Let's pretend that there are two funds, Dashed Fund and Dotted Fund. I will graph their pretend performance over a 12-year period in Figure 1. The fund value is on the vertical axis and the year is on the horizontal axis.

Figure 1:

Dashed Fund Value ■ ■ ■   Dotted Fund Value ● ● ●

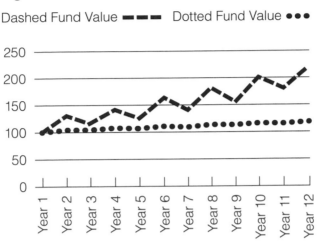

By the way, the data that I used to draw the graph in Figure 1 is provided in Table 4. I want to show you these values, because I want to be fully transparent.

Now, I have a simple question: Which fund would you rather own? Dashed Fund or Dotted Fund? Take a look at Figure 1. Obviously, Dashed Fund looks better, both (1) at the end of the entire 12-year period, and (2) any time during the 12-year period. But guess what:

Dashed Fund's Sharpe ratio = 9.18%/19.26% = 0.48

Dotted Fund's Sharpe ratio = 1.62%/2.31% = 0.70

Table 4:

	Dashed Fund Value	Dotted Fund Value
Year 1	100	100
Year 2	130	104
Year 3	115	103
Year 4	140	107
Year 5	125	106
Year 6	160	110
Year 7	140	109
Year 8	180	113
Year 9	155	112
Year 10	200	116
Year 11	180	115
Year 12	220	119

Based on the returns of the 12 years and based on the standard deviation of those returns, Dotted Fund has a higher Sharpe ratio! So, based on Sharpe ratios, you might mistakenly think Dotted Fund is better. Obviously, in this example, Dashed Fund is better.

Finally, as you know by now, I always like to end an argument on a high note. So, here's my high note. Let's go back to Figure 1, and this time let's say Dotted Fund has a 1.5% annual returns with 0% standard deviation. This is a Sharpe ratio of positive infinity! To see the new comparison between Dotted Fund and Dashed Fund, look at Figure 2.

Figure 2:

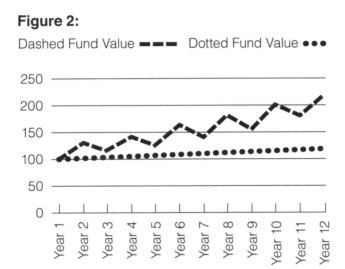

Dashed Fund Value ▬ ▬ ▬ Dotted Fund Value ● ● ●

Even though Dotted Fund has an infinitely larger Sharpe ratio than Dashed Fund, is Dotted Fund the better portfolio in Figure 2? Obviously not. And before you say that there is no such thing as an investment with 0% standard deviation in the real-world (which would be going off tangent, by the way), consider that CDs offered by commercial banks are often FDIC insured, which means that the risk is pretty much 0%. As of this writing, the returns on most one-year CDs currently being offered by commercial banks are less than 1% per year.[63] Wow, that's tiny. Really tiny. If you buy a $100,000 CD, you're only going to end up with a few hundred dollars after an entire year. But because their risk is essentially 0%, this means that these CDs have Sharpe ratios of positive infinity. Are these CDs super-duper awesome investments? Again, if you believe that high Sharpe ratios imply better investments, then this means that these CDs are super-duper awesome investments. But obviously these CDs are not super-duper awesome investments.

Need I say more on this topic? Higher Sharpe ratios, in and of themselves, do not necessarily imply better investments. Wait, did you hear that? That was a high note. It was probably so high that you couldn't even hear it.

Chapter 5a Endnotes:

[60] Christian. (2009, March 15). Ah, yes let's dismiss the Sharpe ratio. Retrieved from http://www.investorgeeks.com/articles/2009/03/15/ah-yes-lets-dismiss-the-sharpe-ratio.

[61] Sharpe ratio. (n.d.). Retrieved from http://www.investopedia.com/terms/s/sharperatio.asp.

[62] U.S. Department of the Treasury. (n.d.). Daily treasury yield curve rates. Accessed July 18, 2014.

[63] I looked up CD rates on bankcd.com on August 15, 2014. The highest available rate on a one-year FDIC-insured CD was 1.09%.

Chapter Six
Mutual funds can lack transparency

Whew, that last chapter was long and technical. I'll give you a break and make this chapter a short one.

You may have heard that mutual funds are not transparent. What does "transparent" mean? First, hidden fees (discussed in Chapter 3) are not "transparent" because you don't really know what's behind all the fees and expenses a mutual fund charges. Second, as explained below, you don't know what stocks are in the mutual funds. Which of these are more unbelievable to you? It's hard to pick, right? Because both are so unbelievable. Anyway, that concludes this chapter—

well, not really. But I've made my point and so, if you want, you can go to the next chapter, but if you want a little bit more elaboration on the two statements above, then you can stay in this chapter for a few more minutes.

Regarding the first point, have you ever tried to buy a mutual fund? If you have, then were you confused about what fees you were paying? There are expense ratios, which consist of management fees, 12b-1 fees, and administrative costs. Those 12b-1 fees can include advertising fees.[64]

Huh? You're paying for the mutual fund to advertise itself? Yes, you are. You've probably seen many pamphlets and television commercials and print advertisements for mutual funds. And yet, have you ever seen an ad that said, "You should buy IBM stocks" or "You should buy Apple stocks." No, you haven't. Seems weird right? Stocks as investments don't advertise themselves. And yet, mutual funds as investments do. Then there may be front-end loads and back-end loads. What are all these costs? It can be confusing. I think the mutual fund industry gets away with charging all of these fees because investors don't understand what they are paying for.[65]

By the way, don't forget that these fees that mutual funds charge are only the disclosed part of the costs of mutual funds. Much of the costs to mutual funds can be undisclosed or "hidden." Remember? From Chapter 3?

Regarding the second point, mutual funds are required by regulations to report their holdings only on a quarterly basis.[66] But other than these four times per year, you usually won't know what stocks are in your fund.[67] Even if you directly asked the mutual fund manager, he or she probably won't tell you what's in the fund.[68] A mutual fund manager might insist that he or she doesn't want to tip off other fund managers of his or her stock picks.[69] To me, this is strange because if we are allowed to see the portfolio contents a few times per year, then what's the harm of seeing them whenever we want to? And, besides, isn't it *your* mutual fund? Isn't this strange? YOU own something, and yet you don't even know what's in it. (By the way, if this is okay with you, then I have a sealed cardboard box that I'd like to sell to you for $1,000. Haha, not really, I wouldn't do that to you, and I don't think you would do that to anyone either, right?) And in between these quarterly holdings reports, the mutual fund may buy and sell stocks without you knowing about it. They could buy a stock, watch it sink, and then quickly sell it before the next quarterly holdings report so that you won't know that the fund had made a bad stock pick. Wait, are mutual funds that sneaky? Yes, they can be. Read the next chapter.

Chapter 6 Endnotes:

[64] Shurr, S. (2003, August 13). False advertising: The truth about 12b-1 fees. Retrieved from http://www.thestreet.com/story/10107579 /1/false-advertising-the-truth-about-12b-1-fees.html.

[65] Mutual fund. (n.d.). Retrieved from http://www.investopedia.com/terms/m/mutualfund.asp.

[66] U.S. Securities and Exchange Commission. (2004, May 10). *Final rule: Shareholder reports and quarterly portfolio disclosure of registered management investment companies.* Retrieved from https://www.sec.gov/rules/final/33-8393.htm.

[67] Rachleff, A. (2011, January 25). Demand transparency in an opaque mutual fund world. *Advisor Perspectives*, 8(4). Retrieved from http://www.advisorperspectives.com/newsletters11/Demand_Transparency_in_an_Opaque_Mutual_Fund_World.php.

[68] Dietz, D. (2000, April 26). What's the big secret about mutual fund holdings? Retrieved from http://www.thestreet.com/story/925755/1/whats-the-big-secret-about-mutual-fund-holdings.html.

[69] Dietz (2000).

Chapter Seven
Mutual funds
can be sneaky

There are many mutual funds out there, and they are competing to get your money. So, maybe it should come as no surprise that they may engage in some questionable behavior to get your business. You might be thinking that maybe they're just pushing the limits to get you some extra profit. Hahaha, no, it's not like that at all. Most of questionable behavior that I am talking about is to TRICK YOU! There are so many sneaky things that mutual funds can do that it's hard to decide which of them to describe and where to start. I'll just describe a few sneaky things that they can do, and I'll begin with incubation.

Incubation

Mutual funds will oftentimes use their own money to start new funds before they make them available to investors. This practice is called "incubation."[70] In theory, this sounds like a great idea. You know, test something out before making it available to the public. This is what pharmaceutical drug companies do. They test drugs before they sell them. In fact, we want drug companies to do this! However, here's the sad thing. These mutual fund companies can use incubation to trick you. Let me explain how.

Let's say, hypothetically, that two funds are newly created, where each fund contains randomly chosen stocks. Based on randomness, we could say that there is a 25% chance that both funds underperform the market (this is like saying there is a 25% chance we get two tails on two coin flips), a 25% chance that both funds outperform the market, and a 50% chance that only one fund outperforms the market (this is like saying that, on two coin flips, there's a 25% chance you get heads then tails, and a 25% chance that you get tails then heads, so there's a 50% chance of getting one head on two coin flips). Now, did you notice something? There is a 75% chance that at least one out of two funds will *randomly* outperform the market! That is, there is a 50% chance that one fund will outperform plus 25% chance that both funds will outperform. In fact, flip a coin two times right now. There's a 75% chance that you'll get heads at least once. Now, at this point, you might be thinking "so what?" Here's the so what....

A mutual fund manager could start two funds in incubation, knowing that the odds are great that at least one fund will *randomly* end up being an outperformer. When a fund randomly outperforms, the fund manager could then make this fund available to investors and could openly publish a "history" of outperformance. Hahaha, that's funny. Now, as an investor, wouldn't you think that the mutual fund manager is great at picking stocks and would this "history" of outperformance influence your decision on whether to buy the fund? If you knew that the fund's outperformance was random, how would that impact your decision? And by the way, those funds that do *not* outperform in incubation may not be made available to the public, and so investors may never know that they ever existed.[71] So, the truth is that the fund manager may just sell incubated funds that randomly did well during incubation, but he or she does not demonstrate special knowledge about stock selection.

Sometimes, an incubated fund that is newly made available to investors might even boast of four consecutive quarters of outperformance. This performance seems impressive, right? But there is actually a 6.25% chance (this is 1 out of 16) that a fund can randomly outperform for four consecutive quarters! So, by creating 16 funds in incubation, there is a good chance that one of them will randomly outperform for four consecutive quarters.[72]

Maybe you think that I'm being cynical. After all, it is entirely possible that incubation is truly a good way to "test" a fund before making it publicly available. Indeed, this is probably how mutual funds pitch this practice.[73] But if this were truly the case, then these so-called "tested" funds should prove to be good after investors buy them, right? Well, I'm sorry to say that it has already been proven that incubated period's outperformance returns were truly random and not indicative of superior managers or strategies by the managers.[74] Specifically, these incubated funds subsequently *underperformed* after they were made available to investors.[75] This is actually not surprising. Stock prices that randomly increase due to no observable fundamental reason should, statistically, tend to decrease over time. Such behavior is known as "mean reversion" to statisticians. Here's a better way to describe what I'm trying to say. Let's say that you give me a basketball and I make two free throws in a row. Am

I good at basketball, or did I get lucky? I'll tell you the truth. I got lucky. So, the odds that I miss my next two free throws are very high. That's what I mean by mean reversion. When positive stock returns occur randomly for no fundamental reason but just occurs based on luck, statistically, those positive returns are unlikely to occur again.

Incubation sounds inappropriate and deceptive, right? Well, this deceptive practice is so well known among finance academics, that we are told to adjust for these contrived incubation returns whenever we analyze and study mutual fund performance.[76] Specifically, we're advised to ignore them! For example, in a white paper by two professors at New York University, they state,

> There are problems with returns data that a researcher must be aware of. First is the problem of backfill bias most often associated with incubator funds.... This causes an upward bias in mutual fund return data.... This bias

can be controlled for in two ways. First, when a fund goes public it gets a ticker. Eliminating all data before the ticker creation eliminates the bias. Second, eliminating the first three years of history for all funds also eliminates the bias.[77]

In other words, incubator funds' historical returns are so meaningless that they should be ignored.

Feel tricked, right? Here are additional ways that mutual funds try to trick you.

Window dressing

Now remember that mutual fund returns and holdings are usually made available on a quarterly basis. To help prepare for those quarterly events, mutual funds might try to "window dress" or make things appear rosier than they really are. Here's two examples of window dressing.

Remember "price impact" from earlier in this book? This is where stock prices can increase simply because of the large demand for the stock and for no other fundamental reason. Well, if I'm a mutual fund manager and I anticipate that my mutual fund's performance for the upcoming quarter is not going to look great, you know what I could do? I could buy a lot more shares of stocks that my fund *already* owns to inflate those stock prices! Yep, this is already being done.[78,79] This is called "leaning for the tape." You know, this is what runners do in a sprint race. This practice is fine for them because the finish line is the end of the race. But for mutual funds and for most investors, the quarters are not the end. You want to remain in the game, or you wouldn't be reading this book. Don't forget that this price increase from "price impact" has been shown to be only temporary. But the costs (commissions, bid–ask spreads, and the artificially inflated cost paid for the stock) can be a drag on total returns.[80]

Another form of window-dressing is the following. Let's say that a fund holds Dumb stock but not Smart stock. During the quarter, let's say that Dumb stock does really poorly and Smart stock does really great (haha, just based on the stock names alone, you could have predicted this). Now, given this situation, the fund manager probably feels pretty ashamed of himself. And he probably doesn't want anyone to find out about his poor stock selection. Uh-oh, the quarterly reporting is coming up! Quick, get rid of Dumb stock and buy Smart stock! This could hide the bad stock selection! The investors of the funds may never find out. In fact, to the investors, the manager may even look smart. They might think that the manager held Smart stock all along, and never held Dumb stock. Yep, this happens.[81]

Remember, window-dressing is done to FOOL YOU!

Not tricks but just some other inappropriate things that some mutual funds do

You likely are getting the point, so, I will just quickly

describe a few other inappropriate things that mutual funds do and wrap this up.

Excessive risk-taking near the quarter-end

As a quarter comes to a close, your mutual fund's returns might be comparable to market returns. As an investor, this is probably just fine with you. But for the mutual fund manager, this is likely nothing to brag about. In fact, he or she may even feel like he or she is not doing his or her job well. So, the manager might take a bunch of excessive risks near the quarter-end, to see if he or she can boost the fund's returns a bit.[82] This excessive risk-taking usually won't pay off. For the fund manager, this may be no big deal, as he or she had nothing to brag about to begin with, and he or she still has nothing to brag about. But the manager's excessive risk-taking might have caused your fund's returns to be below market returns!

Favoritism toward institutional clients

When institutional investors invest in mutual funds, they might actually be getting their money's worth. They usually pay lower fees and the mutual fund manager will work hard to achieve outperformance for the institutional client.[83] Eh, not surprising. Maybe you'd do the same thing if you were a mutual fund manager. You know, you want to impress the big clients. You want them to be happy. They're the big and sophisticated investors, after all. But if the mutual fund that you are investing in does not have institutional clients, then the fund manager may not be working so hard, or he or she may be neglecting your fund while he or she focuses on other funds with institutional clients.

Helping their investment banking business

When a mutual fund is affiliated with an investment bank, the fund manager may buy some of the IPOs that the investment bank underwrote if other investors didn't buy up the entire offering.[84] Jeez, I can just picture this.

Investment banker: "I need a drink."

Mutual fund manager: "Why, what's up?"

Investment banker: "The IPO that I underwrote is not getting bought up. I guess I was wrong about bringing that firm public or maybe the offer price was too high. I don't know. I'm going to be screwed, maybe fired."

Mutual fund manager: "Don't worry. I'll use some of my fund's money to buy the remaining shares you got left over."

Investment banker: "Really? You'd do that for me?"

Mutual fund manager: "Not for you, but for the firm. We work at the same firm, you idiot."

Investment banker: "That's awesome. Now I'm in the mood for a celebration drink. Let's go. I'm buying!"

Conclusion to the chapter

Mutual funds can be sneaky.

Chapter 7 Endnotes:

[70] Evans, R. B. (2010). Mutual fund incubation. *Journal of Finance*, 66, 1581–1611.

[71] Evans (2010).

[72] There's a 50% chance that you will get heads on a coin flip. You get this probability; it's just 0.5n = 50% when n = number of coin flips = 1. The probability that you will get heads four times on four coin flips is 0.54 = 6.25%.

[73] I want to cite examples of this, but I don't want to single out any specific mutual fund and make my compliance officer nervous. I'll let you Google it. By the way, many mutual funds often describe incubated funds as "limited distribution" funds (see www.investopedia.com/terms/i/incubatedfund.asp) and so use this term when Googling: Incubated fund. (n.d.). Retrieved from http://www.investopedia.com/ terms/i/ incubatedfund.asp.

[74] Evans (2010).

[75] Evans (2010).

[76] Elton, E. J., & Gruber, M. J. (2011). Mutual funds. Working paper, New York University. Retrieved from http://pages.stern.nyu.edu/~eelton/Mutual% 20Funds4-13-11.pdf.

[77] Elton and Gruber (2010).

[78] Agarwal, V., Gay, G. D., & Ling, L. (2013, July 26). Window dressing in mutual funds. SSRN working paper.

[79] Carhart, M. M., Kaniel, R., Musto, D. K., & Reed, A. V. (2002). Leaning for the tape: Evidence of gaming behavior in equity mutual funds. *Journal of Finance*, 57, 661–693.

[80] Ultimate guide to retirement. (n.d.). Retrieved from http://money.cnn.com/ retirement/guide/investing_mutualfunds.moneymag/index14.htm.

[81] Ro, S. (2012, September 26). The truth about "window dressing": How some portfolio managers try to dupe their clients at the end of every quarter. Retrieved from http:// www.businessinsider.com/yes-window-dressing-occurs-but-the-window-dressers-are-

taking-a-huge-risk-2012-9.

[82] Huang, J., Sialm, C., & Zhang, H. (2011). Risk shifting and mutual fund performance. *Review of Financial Studies*, 24, 2575–2616.

[83] Evans, R. B., & Fahlenbrach, R. (2012). Institutional investors and mutual fund governance: Evidence from retail–institutional fund twins. *Review of Financial Studies*, 25, 3530–3571.

[84] Hao, Q., & Yan, X. (2012). The performance of investment bank-affiliated mutual funds: Conflicts of interest or informational advantage? *Journal of Financial and Quantitative Analysis*, 47, 537–565.

Chapter Eight
A simple straightforward alternative

Don't you just hate it when people complain but have no idea how to make things better? I'm sometimes guilty of that. But in this case, I actually do know of an alternative to mutual funds that I believe is better. It's simple. Hire your very own money manager and have him or her pick and buy stocks, just for you. This way you can directly and literally own the stocks and obtain the benefits of portfolio diversification, all without having to bear the costs of commingled investors. This is how the likes of wealthy investors, university endowments, and many large institutions invest.[85] If you invest this way, then you likely won't be affected by the tax inefficiency that I described in Chapter 2, nor would you be affected by the transactions costs induced by other investors (i.e., the undisclosed "hidden" costs) that I described in Chapter 3. These kinds of accounts that I'm talking about are known as separately managed accounts (SMAs).

The historical problem is that you may not be wealthy enough to have access to a money manager or to an SMA. While that might have been true in the 20th century, that's not true anymore. Many financial advisors today are now offering the opportunity for people like you and me to invest just like wealthy individuals by providing us with separately managed accounts at a low cost and at low account minimums that we can afford. Over the past decade or so, the technology has improved dramatically to help make it easy to get access to professional money managers through separately managed accounts.

In fact, why not outdo rich people and have access to a bunch of money managers, where one might specialize in picking large cap stocks, another specializing in selecting value stocks, and even a different manager whose expertise lies in the area of fixed income strategies. Or better yet, why not have access to several money managers that specialize in large cap stocks and have the option of choosing the money manager that you think is the best one at picking large cap stocks. This is possible with today's technology and low costs. Of course, you don't need to make the tough decisions of which money managers to choose. Your financial advisor can do this for you. He or she can select different money managers to help manage your different portfolio of stocks.

The technology provided by my firm also helps drive down money management costs and administrative costs. We can pass the cost savings along to financial advisors so that they can pass the savings along to their clients. These advisors can then pick multiple money managers to make the actual stock selections. And these are not just any money managers. My firm, for example, carefully screens them (based on their performance, investment strategies, and their management) to help make sure that they satisfy our high standards of performance and investment philosophy.

So, using our technology, an advisor along with her or his client could sit down and create a separately managed account that replicates the stock selections of many money managers. Maybe the advisor's client will go with Manager Bob's stock selection of large cap stocks, go with Manager Sue's stock selection of value stocks, and go with Manager Jill's stock selection of emerging market stocks. Isn't this great? Having all of these money managers, in effect, managing your money. And your advisor can help with you this, because we provide the technology that can make all of this possible.

Are you ready to consider your very own separately managed account? Then there's just one more chapter to read.

Chapter 8 Endnotes:

[85] Singh, M. How to invest like an endowment. (n.d.). Retrieved from http://www.investopedia.com/articles/financial-theory/09/ivy-league-endowments-money-management.asp.

Chapter Nine
Learning more and a next step

Okay, by now you have formed an opinion as to whether mutual funds are an appropriate way for you to invest, and you may want to know what to do next. Actually, the next step is simple. I think you should contact your financial advisor and make sure you are not in mutual funds! Talk to her or him about investing in separately managed accounts (SMAs) or unified managed accounts (UMAs) and how you can get started investing this way.

If you or your advisor want to learn more, then you

or your advisor can contact my firm, EQIS Capital directly. If you need an advisor, we can also help identify financial advisors with access to money managers and administrative support to help keep your costs low. There is usually an EQIS-affiliated financial advisor near you. EQIS can also administer a Mutual Fund Stress Test for you, to see how much your current mutual funds might be costing you. You can also contact us at 800-949-9936 and schedule a 30-minute appointment with one of our professionals to learn more about the EQIS advantage.

Kenneth A. Kim, PhD

Dr. Kenneth A. Kim has been a finance professor for 20 years. He has taught at 16 different universities including the State University of New York at Buffalo, Georgetown University, and the University of Michigan. He has spent his entire academic career exposing inefficiencies in financial markets and in financial industry through his writing and research (his many academic papers appear in prestigious academic journals such as the Journal of Finance, Journal of Business, Journal of Financial Markets, and Journal of Financial Intermediation) and through his teaching (one of his teaching awards was given to him by the governor of Wisconsin and another by the chancellor of the State University of New York system). His desire and dedication to protect and to help individual investors led to an appointment as a senior financial economist for the U.S. Securities and Exchange Commission in Washington,

DC, during the late 1990s. Dr. Kim has been quoted or his research has been cited in numerous print and online media, including the Wall Street Journal, BusinessWeek, NewsWeek, New York Times, Washington Post, Boston Globe, MSNBC.com, TheStreet.com, Kiplingers.com, Fidelity.com, CNBC, MSN News, CBS Radio, and National Public Radio. Dr. Kim is now Chief Financial Strategist at EQIS Capital Management.

William R. Nelson, PhD

Dr. William R. Nelson has been the EQIS's Chief Investment Officer for the past 10 years. As a former member of the Chicago Board of Trade and a former professor of economics at the State University of New York at Buffalo, Dr. Nelson uses a unique blend of industry experience and academic rigor in managing (or co-managing with Dr. Kim) EQIS portfolios. For example, a guiding principle that Dr. Nelson employs in his security selection is the rigorous and methodological Porter's Five Forces Model. When Dr. Nelson was an academic scholar, his primary research (which was published in prestigious journals such as the American Economic Review, Journal of Economic Behavior and Organizations, and Public Choice) focused on how fairness and fair play affect decision-making, choices, and outcomes and on how to mitigate corrupt behavior. These research interests were spawned from his life-long passion for fairness and fair outcomes, which is why he was particularly keen on coauthoring a book that exposes mutual fund flaws.

Index

Notes:

Notes: